From *The Together Book*, illustrated by Roger Bradfield, 1971.

Love the Fur You're In

Our sincere gratitude to the artists or their estates who generously and graciously gave permission to use their illustrations in this book.

To the artists whose work is represented here, and to every artist who has illustrated *Sesame Street* books over the years—honorary *Sesame Street* Monsters all: Through your imaginative, humorous, and loving interpretations of these icons, you have brought to lasting life a unique cast of characters and, in the process, have become timeless icons yourselves. You are now, and ever will be, a part of the lives of the many generations who grew up with *Sesame Street,* and of those still to come. Thank you.

The editors also would like to thank those at Sesame Workshop, Random House, and points far and near who helped in myriad ways in the making of this book.

Visit us on the Web!
rhcbooks.com
www.sesamestreet.org

Educators and librarians, for a variety of teaching tools, visit us at RHTeachersLibrarians.com

ISBN 978-0-593-37767-3 (Proprietary Edition)

MANUFACTURED IN GUANGDONG PROVINCE, CHINA
January 2021
10 9 8 7 6 5 4 3 2 1

Exclusive Proprietary Edition 2021

SESAME STREET

Love the Fur You're In

MONSTER WIT AND WISDOM

WITH ART FROM 50 YEARS OF SESAME STREET BOOKS

Random House 🏠 New York

You're always welcome on Sesame Street.

From *I Think That It Is Wonderful*, illustrated by A. Delaney, 1984.

The only thing better than a hug is a running hug!

From *Big Bird and Little Bird's Big & Little Book*, second edition, illustrated by A. Delaney, 1983.

Find someone who can dance
to your tune.

From *Ernie & Bert Can . . . Can You?*, illustrated by Michael Smollin, 1982.

Believe!

From *Elmo and Abby's Wacky Weather Day*, illustrated by Tom Brannon, 2011.

From *Ernie's Big Mess*, illustrated by Joe Mathieu, 1981.

Pick your battles—and your roommates—carefully.

Sometimes you need a little space.

From *Can You Tell Me How to Get to Sesame Street?*, illustrated by Joe Mathieu, 1997.

But first, a hug.

From *Monster Places*, illustrated by Tom Brannon, 1996.

Keep calm and cookie on.

From *The Monsters on the Bus*, illustrated by Joe Ewers, 2001.

Go fly a kite.

From *The Sesame Street ABC Book of Words*,
illustrated by Harry McNaught, 1988.

Expect the unexpected.

From *The Sesame Street Storybook*, illustration by Kelli Oechsli, 1971.

Snuggle up with a Snuffalupagus.

From *Oscar's Silly ABC's and Other Stories*, illustrated by Tom Brannon, 1987.

Read the instructions *first.*

From *Sesame Street Talent Show*, illustrated by Joe Ewers, 1997.

Find your purr-fect furry friend.

From *Elmo Can . . . Quack Like a Duck*, illustrated by Maggie Swanson, 1997.

You do you.

And do your 'do.

From *I Can Do It Myself*, illustrated by Richard Brown, 1980.

This is your life—smile!

From *Brought to You by the Number 1*, illustrated by Tom Brannon, 1999.

Fun is waterproof.

From *Splish-Splashy Day*, illustrated by Joe Ewers, 1989.

Surround yourself with things that bring you joy.

From *The Songs of Sesame Street in Poems and Pictures*, illustrated by Normand Chartier, 1983.

Life's an adventure—
but pack a map.

From *Are We There Yet?*, illustrated by Tom Brannon, 1998.

Don't give a hoot—
just play your song.

From *I Am a Bird*, illustrated by Tom Brannon, 1994.

If news spreads fast,
make it good news.

From *Elmo's 12 Days of Christmas*, illustrated by Maggie Swanson, 1996.

There's no such thing as too many books.

ALL your angles are your best angles.

From *I Think That It Is Wonderful*, illustrated by A. Delaney, 1984.

Every dawn is another sunny day.

From *The Sesame Street Book of Poetry*, illustrated by Bruce McNally, 1992.

A good friend makes it all better.

From *Wait for Me!*, illustrated by Joe Mathieu, 1987.

When you have a gift, give it to others.

Make a wish!

From *Sesame Street Story Land*, illustration by Tom Cooke, 1986.

Swing for the fences.

From *Give It a Try, Zoe!*, illustrated by Tom Brannon, 2002.

Some days call for more than one scoop.

From *The Day the Count Stopped Counting*, illustrated by Michael Smollin, 1977.

Love the fur you're in.

From *The Monster at the End of This Book*,
illustrated by Michael Smollin, 1971.

Sing like no one's listening.

From *I Am a Bird*, illustrated by Tom Brannon, 1994.

Express yourself!

From *My Name Is Elmo*, illustrated by Maggie Swanson, 1993.

Physics 101 really is important!

From *The Sesame Street Storybook*, illustration by Michael Frith, 1971.

Just breathe.

**A good friend checks
your tail feathers
for you.**

From *The Together Book*, illustrated by Roger Bradfield, 1971.

You're never too old for story time.

From *The Sesame Street Library* series, endpaper illustration by Joe Mathieu, 1970s.

Dive into a good book.

From B *Is for Books*, illustrated by Joe Mathieu, 1996.

Always wear clean underwear!

From *The Sesame Street ABC Book of Words*, illustrated by Harry McNaught, 1988.

Don't bury your feelings.

From *The Monster at the End of This Book*, illustrated by Michael Smollin, 1971.

Just roll with it.

From *The Together Book*, illustrated by Roger Bradfield, 1971.

Don't hide your light under a trash can lid.

From *Oscar's Book*, illustrated by Michael Gross, 1975.

**Follow the Monsters—
they know the way.**

From *Follow the Monsters!*, illustrated by Tom Cooke, 1985.

Never underestimate the superpower of a nap.

From *What Ernie and Bert Did on Their Summer Vacation*, illustrated by Joe Mathieu, 1977.

Wherever you go,
go with a friend.

From *The Sesame Street Storybook*, illustration by Mary Lou Dettmer, 1971.

Don't count your cookies until they're baked.

From *The Day the Count Stopped Counting*, illustrated by Michael Smollin, 1977.

Can't bear it?
Share it!

From *The Together Book*, illustrated by Roger Bradfield, 1971.

Don't get frazzled!

Stop and smell the flowers.

From *The Sesame Street Book of Poetry*, illustrated by Bruce McNally, 1992.

Slow down before you fall down.

From *Monster Places*, illustrated by Tom Brannon, 1996.

Everyone has a story.

From the Sesame Street Start-to-Read series, endpaper illustration by Joe Mathieu, 1980s.

You really are a masterpiece.

From *The Sesame Street 1, 2, 3 Storybook*, illustration by Bob Taylor, 1973.

La música es el lenguaje del amor.

From *Brought to You by . . . Sesame Street!*, illustration by Richard Walz, 2004.

North, south, east, or west . . .

From *The Sesame Street 1976 Calendar,* illustrated by Michael Smollin.

. . . go where your dreams take you.

Go on—rain is good for your fur.

From *Splish-Splashy Day*, illustrated by Joe Ewers, 1989.

Always have a Plan B.
And also a Plan C.
And maybe a Plan D . . . E . . . F . . .

From *We're Counting on You, Grover!*, illustrated by Joe Ewers, 1991.

From *Imagination Song*, illustrated by Laurent Linn, 2001.

Follow your Rubber Duckie.

Rx: Laughter (the best medicine).

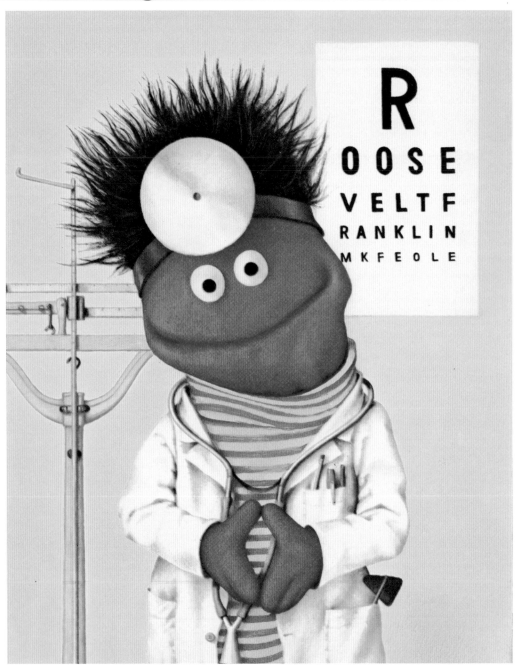

From *Muppets in My Neighborhood*, illustrated by Harry McNaught, 1977.

Focus. Just . . . focus.

From *The Sesame Street ABC Book of Words*, illustrated by Harry McNaught, 1988.

Friends can help you weather any storm.

From *A My Name Is Alice*, illustrated by Joe Mathieu, 1989.

From *Muppets in My Neighborhood*, illustrated by Harry McNaught, 1977.

When a wrench will work,
leave the blowtorch in the box.

The secret to a happy life is balance.

From *I Am a Bird*, illustrated by Tom Brannon, 1994.

Always pack your essentials.

From *Ernie's Big Mess*, illustrated by Joe Mathieu, 1981.

Shoot for the moon!

From *Slimey to the Moon*, illustrated by Richard Walz, 1999.

Imagination can take you anywhere.

From *Oscar's Book*, illustrated by Michael Gross, 1975.

Be someone's Super Grover.

From *The Exciting Adventures of Super Grover*, illustrated by Joe Mathieu, 1978.

Dance, flutter, and fly.

From *Imagination Song*, illustrated by Laurent Linn, 2001.

Just hold on!

From *The Sesame Street Dictionary*, illustrated by Joe Mathieu, 1980.

Lend an ear.
(The one without the banana in it.)

Heroes come in all shapes and sizes.

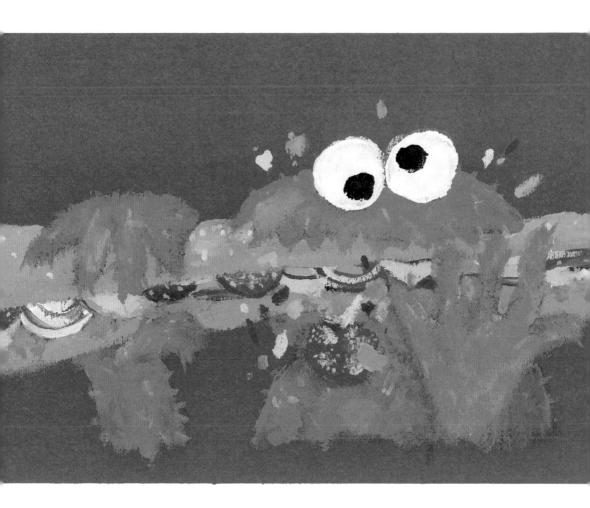

From *Food! by Cookie Monster*, illustrated by Mike Pantuso, 2002.

**Sometimes the answer you get
is not the answer you want.**

From *The Sesame Street Dictionary*, illustrated by Joe Mathieu, 1980.

Life isn't always a straight line.

From *In & Out, Up & Down*, illustrated by Michael Smollin, 1982.

Be your own director.

From *The Day the Count Stopped Counting*, illustrated by Michael Smollin, 1977.

Don't miss what's right under your nose.

From *Sesame Street 1 2 3: A Counting Book from 1 to 100*, illustrated by Joe Mathieu, 1991.

Find your own recipe for fun.

From *The Case of the Missing Duckie*, illustrated by Maggie Swanson, 1980.

Done is better than perfect.

From *The Sesame Street Dictionary*, illustrated by Joe Mathieu, 1980.

Remember, you're *always* welcome on Sesame Street.

From *I Think That It Is Wonderful*, illustrated by A. Delaney, 1984.

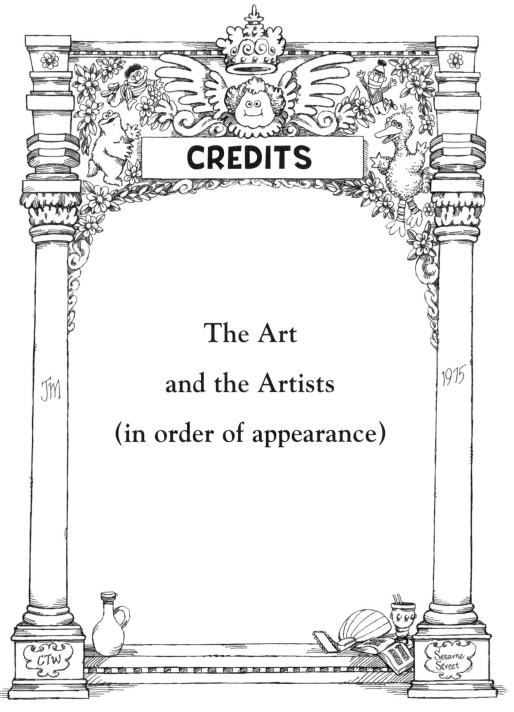

CREDITS

The Art

and the Artists

(in order of appearance)

Pages 2–3: Sesame Street, early days, from *The Sesame Street Storybook*, endpaper illustration by Michael Frith, 1971.

Pages 4–5: Sesame Street scene, from *The Together Book*, illustrated by Roger Bradfield, 1971.

Page 7: Big Bird dancing, from *The Sesame Street Storybook*, illustration by Michael Frith, 1971.

Page 8: Barkley asleep on stoop, dawn, from *I Think That It Is Wonderful*, illustrated by A. Delaney, 1984.

Page 9: Big Bird and Little Bird, from *Big Bird and Little Bird's Big & Little Book*, second edition, illustrated by A. Delaney, 1983.

Page 10: Bert dancing to Ernie's tune, from *Ernie & Bert Can . . . Can You?*, illustrated by Michael Smollin, 1982.

Page 11: Abby making magic, from *Elmo and Abby's Wacky Weather Day*, illustrated by Tom Brannon, 2011.

Pages 12–13: Bert and Ernie in messy room, from *Ernie's Big Mess*, illustrated by Joe Mathieu, 1981.

Page 14: Elmo on the magic carpet, from *Can You Tell Me How to Get to Sesame Street?*, illustrated by Joe Mathieu, 1997.

Page 15: Grover and Mommy hugging, from *Monster Places*, illustrated by Tom Brannon, 1996.

Pages 16–17: Martians on the bus, from *The Monsters on the Bus*, illustrated by Joe Ewers, 2001.

Pages 18–19: Gang flying kites, from *The Sesame Street ABC Book of Words*, illustrated by Harry McNaught, 1988.

Page 20: Cookie and the genie, from *The Sesame Street Storybook*, illustration by Kelli Oechsli, 1971.

Page 21: Gang reading with Snuffy, from *Oscar's Silly ABC's and Other Stories*, illustrated by Tom Brannon, 1987.

Page 22: Mumford in a magic mess, from *Sesame Street Talent Show*, illustrated by Joe Ewers, 1997.

Page 23: Elmo and kitty, from *Elmo Can . . . Quack Like a Duck*, illustrated by Maggie Swanson, 1997.

Pages 24–25: Ernie and Bert combing hair, from *I Can Do It Myself*, illustrated by Richard Brown, 1980.

Pages 26–27: Guy Smiley and friends, from *Brought to You by the Number 1*, illustrated by Tom Brannon, 1999.

Page 28: Gang jumping in puddles, from *Splish-Splashy Day*, illustrated by Joe Ewers, 1989.

Page 29: Oscar with favorite trash, from *The Songs of Sesame Street in Poems and Pictures*, illustrated by Normand Chartier, 1983.

Page 30: Zoe with a map, from *Are We There Yet?*, illustrated by Tom Brannon, 1998.

Page 31: Hoots with his saxophone, from *I Am a Bird*, illustrated by Tom Brannon, 1994.

Pages 32–33: Elmo and Anything Monsters talking on the phone, from *Elmo's 12 Days of Christmas*, illustrated by Maggie Swanson, 1996.

Page 34: Elmo with a stack of books, from *1, 2, 3 by Elmo*, illustrated by Mike Pantuso, 2002.

Page 35: Snuffy, from *I Think That It Is Wonderful*, illustrated by A. Delaney, 1984.

Page 36: Big Bird at dawn, from *The Sesame Street Book of Poetry*, illustrated by Bruce McNally, 1992.

Page 37: Grover bandaging Elmo's knee, from *Wait for Me!*, illustrated by Joe Mathieu, 1987.

Pages 38–39: Gang on the *Anna Jane*, from *The Exciting Adventures of Super Grover*, illustrated by Joe Mathieu, 1978.

Page 40: Grover playing violin, from *The Sesame Street ABC Book of Words*, illustrated by Harry McNaught, 1988.

Page 41: Big Bird, Elmo, and Snuffy wishing on a star, from *Sesame Street Story Land,* illustration by Tom Cooke, 1986.

Page 42: Zoe batting, from *Give It a Try, Zoe!,* illustrated by Tom Brannon, 2002.

Page 43: Ernie with lots of ice cream, from *The Day the Count Stopped Counting,* illustrated by Michael Smollin, 1977.

Page 44: Grover hugging himself, from *The Monster at the End of This Book,* illustrated by Michael Smollin, 1971.

Page 45: Big Bird "singing," from *I Am a Bird,* illustrated by Tom Brannon, 1994.

Pages 46–47: Elmo making faces, from *My Name Is Elmo,* illustrated by Maggie Swanson, 1993.

Pages 48–49: Cookie and cookie catapult, from *The Sesame Street Storybook,* illustration by Michael Frith, 1971.

Page 50: Grover meditating, from *Imagine . . . Grover's Magic Carpet Ride,* illustrated by Tom Brannon, 1993.

Page 51: Big Bird and Snuffy, from *The Together Book,* illustrated by Roger Bradfield, 1971.

Pages 52–53: Sesame friends reading, from *The Sesame Street Library* series, endpaper illustration by Joe Mathieu, 1970s.

Page 54: Slimey in an apple, from *B Is for Books,* illustrated by Joe Mathieu, 1996.

Page 55: Bert on doctor's scale, from *The Sesame Street ABC Book of Words,* illustrated by Harry McNaught, 1988.

Pages 56–57: Grover under the bricks, from *The Monster at the End of This Book,* illustrated by Michael Smollin, 1971.

Page 58: Roosevelt Franklin and friend, from *The Together Book,* illustrated by Roger Bradfield, 1971.

Page 59: Oscar hiding in a stack of cans, from *Oscar's Book,* illustrated by Michael Gross, 1975.

Pages 60–61: Shadow Monsters, from *Follow the Monsters!,* illustrated by Tom Cooke, 1985.

Page 62: Grover napping under an apple tree, from *What Ernie and Bert Did on Their Summer Vacation,* illustrated by Joe Mathieu, 1977.

Page 63: Herry and friend, from *The Sesame Street Storybook,* illustration by Mary Lou Dettmer, 1971.

Page 64: The Count counting Cookie's cookies, from *The Day the Count Stopped Counting,* illustrated by Michael Smollin, 1977.

Page 65: Betty Lou with giant pudding, from *The Together Book,* illustrated by Roger Bradfield, 1971.

Page 66: Frazzle, from *The Sesame Street Dictionary,* illustrated by Joe Mathieu, 1980.

Page 67: Big Bird smelling the flowers, from *The Sesame Street Book of Poetry,* illustrated by Bruce McNally, 1992.

Pages 68–69: Grover getting dizzy, from *Monster Places,* illustrated by Tom Brannon, 1996.

Pages 70–71: Sesame Street gang reading around stoop of 123, from the Sesame Street Start-to-Read series, endpaper illustration by Joe Mathieu, 1980s.

Page 72: Sherlock Hemlock looking at his portrait, from *The Sesame Street 1, 2, 3 Storybook,* illustration by Bob Taylor, 1973.

Page 73: Rosita, from *Brought to You by . . . Sesame Street!,* illustration by Richard Walz, 2004.

Pages 74–75: Grover flying a biplane, from *The Sesame Street 1976 Calendar,* illustrated by Michael Smollin.

Page 76: Honkers in the rain, from *Splish-Splashy Day*, illustrated by Joe Ewers, 1989.

Page 77: Prairie Dawn and Grover in a tizzy, from *We're Counting on You, Grover!*, illustrated by Joe Ewers, 1991.

Pages 78–79: Ernie and Rubber Duckie on a boat, from *Imagination Song*, illustrated by Laurent Linn, 2001.

Page 80: Roosevelt Franklin, MD, from *Muppets in My Neighborhood*, illustrated by Harry McNaught, 1977.

Page 81: Cookie and a wave, from *The Sesame Street ABC Book of Words*, illustrated by Harry McNaught, 1988.

Pages 82–83: Gang under one umbrella, from *A My Name Is Alice*, illustrated by Joe Mathieu, 1989.

Pages 84–85: Grover and Betty Lou as plumbers, from *Muppets in My Neighborhood*, illustrated by Harry McNaught, 1977.

Page 86: Gang on the seesaw, from *I Am a Bird*, illustrated by Tom Brannon, 1994.

Page 87: Ernie packing a suitcase, from *Ernie's Big Mess*, illustrated by Joe Mathieu, 1981.

Pages 88–89: Slimey blasting off, from *Slimey to the Moon*, illustrated by Richard Walz, 1999.

Page 90: Oscar in his spacecraft, from *Oscar's Book*, illustrated by Michael Gross, 1975.

Page 91: Super Grover, from *The Exciting Adventures of Super Grover*, illustrated by Joe Mathieu, 1978.

Pages 92–93: Zoe in butterfly tutu, from *Imagination Song*, illustrated by Laurent Linn, 2001.

Page 94: Rodeo Rosie, from *The Sesame Street Dictionary*, illustrated by Joe Mathieu, 1980.

Page 95: Ernie with banana in his ear, from the *Sesame Street* style guide.

Page 96: Cookie Monster and big sandwich, from *Food! by Cookie Monster*, illustrated by Mike Pantuso, 2002.

Page 97: Grover and "Fat Blue," from *The Sesame Street Dictionary*, illustrated by Joe Mathieu, 1980.

Page 98: Herry painting, from *In & Out, Up & Down*, illustrated by Michael Smollin, 1982.

Page 99: The Count directing, from *The Day the Count Stopped Counting*, illustrated by Michael Smollin, 1977.

Pages 100–101: Ernie and the Twiddlebugs, from *Sesame Street 1 2 3: A Counting Book from 1 to 100*, illustrated by Joe Mathieu, 1991.

Page 102: Sherlock Hemlock and Cookie, from *The Case of the Missing Duckie*, illustrated by Maggie Swanson, 1980.

Page 103: Biff and Sully, from *The Sesame Street Dictionary*, illustrated by Joe Mathieu, 1980.

Page 104: Barkley asleep on stoop, night, from *I Think That It Is Wonderful*, illustrated by A. Delaney, 1984.

Page 105: Black-and-white archway, from *The Sesame Street Book of Fairy Tales*, illustrated by Joe Mathieu, 1975.

Page 109: Gang at sunset, from *The Sesame Street Book of Poetry*, illustrated by Bruce McNally, 1992.

Pages 110–111: Sesame Street, early days, from *The Sesame Street Storybook*, endpaper illustration by Michael Frith, 1971.

Back cover: Gang on the wall, from *The Sesame Street Storybook*, cover illustration by Michael Frith, 1971.

From *The Sesame Street Book of Poetry*, illustrated by Bruce McNally, 1992.

Grover

Will Lee as
Mr. Hooper

Herbert Birdsfoot

Kermit Love,
Muppet builder of
Big Bird, as Willie

Sherlock Hemlock

Roosevelt Franklin
and his mom

Callee, Michael Frith's
oldest daughter

Christina, Michael Frith's
middle child